BOOK ONE

TAKE UP THE FLUTE

BY GRAHAM LYONS

MIDPOINT PRESS
EXCLUSIVE EDITION · EXCLUSIVE EDITION ·

TO THE STUDENT

You already know many of the tunes in this book and you will soon be able to play them all!

Do not worry if you cannot read music because, almost without knowing it, you will build up the skill as you enjoy working through the book. The **Note Recognition Games** and **Rhythm Practices** are fun to try and they will tell you how well you are doing.

Action Replays put the spotlight on potential problems. *Play these very slowly over and over again;* your fingers will quickly learn what to do and you will then be able to play them at the normal speed.

You will get a lot of fun from using this book, but remember that playing the flute is a serious business too. *Practise regularly and carefully follow the instructions of your teacher.* By doing this your playing will steadily improve and you will be able to perform even more of your favourite music.

TO THE TEACHER

The repertoire in **TAKE UP THE FLUTE** has been most carefully chosen. Each tune has a specific teaching function: it may introduce a new note or rhythm, give practice over awkward fingerings, or perhaps promote good tone production, general control and finger dexterity.

Sometimes the explanation of a new notational element is deliberately left until it has been used several times in really well known melodies. The student's aural awareness will initially carry him or her through rhythmic problems; consolidation through theory and exercises comes later.

The graded **Note Recognition Games** and **Rhythm Practices** are designed to help with note reading; there are also plenty of less familiar and original pieces for sight reading.

TAKE UP THE FLUTE is more than a 'fun' book. It provides a sympathetically structured background to each student's natural enthusiasm.

STAGE 1

Hold the **head joint** only.

Place your bottom lip on the **lip plate**, covering about a third of the **blow hole**.

Imagine that you are about to say the word "bee" and blow, aiming your airstream at the far edge of the lip plate.

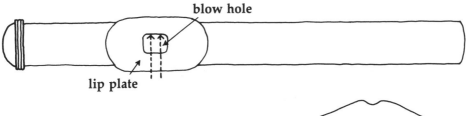

Your mouth shape should look roughly like this (check in a mirror):

Do *not* blow as if smiling or whistling.

Experiment with the sound (if any!) by turning the head joint very slightly towards you or away from you, and also by moving it fractionally to the left or right.

Use long, even breaths, as if you are trying to keep a feather in the air or make ripples on water.

Play loud and soft notes, long and short ones.

When you can achieve a satisfactory sound two times out of three, assemble the flute.

ASSEMBLING THE FLUTE

Hold the flute gently around the keys as you put it together. Too much pressure may damage the mechanism.

Carefully place the head joint into the **middle joint**, and by *gently* twisting and pushing, line up the centre of the blow hole with the first key on the middle section:

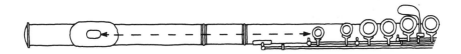

The rod on the **foot joint** should point to the centre of the nearest key on the middle joint. N.B. The rods on these two joints *should not be in line*.

foot joint rod

HOLDING THE FLUTE

Left Hand fingers

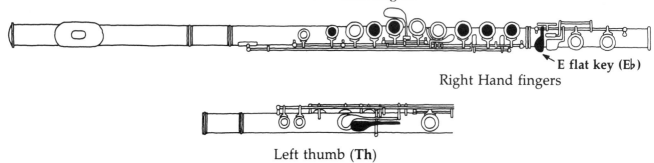

E flat key (E♭)

Right Hand fingers

Left thumb (**Th**)

Hand positions
from the front

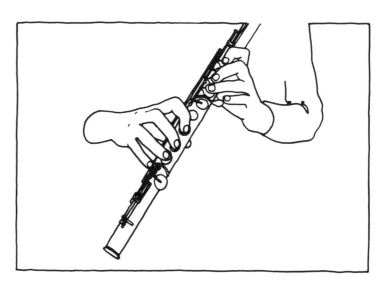

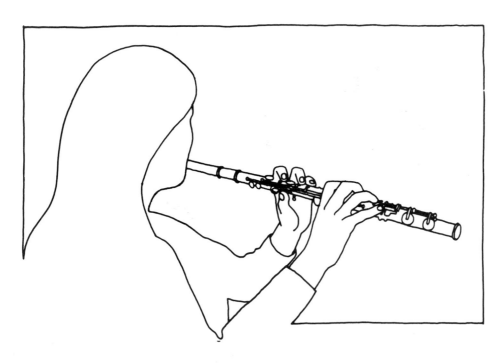

Hand positions
from the back

The first finger is curved into a position that at first feels quite awkward; but the lower part of the finger makes one of the essential support points for the flute.

For a comfortable playing position, *tilt* your head and the flute slightly to the right. Also *turn* your head a little towards your left shoulder. *Always bring the flute up to your lips;* don't bend down to the flute.

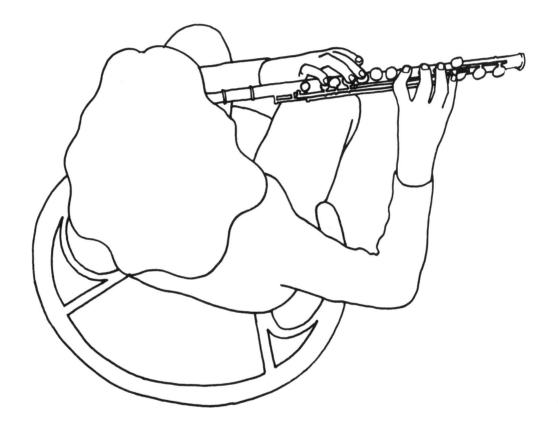

Play the note D:*

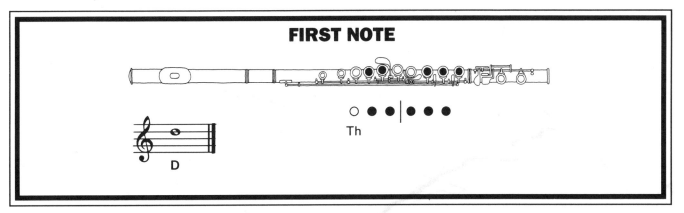

Holding the whole flute in place is obviously more difficult than holding just the head joint. As a result, the blow hole will very likely drift out of position. Constantly check your position *by looking in a mirror*. In fact until you know how to place your lips by "feel", a mirror is invaluable.

Experiment with the position as you did with the head joint – also try loud and soft s, long and short ones. You will get tired; so, quite often, put the flute down, rest for 30 seconds and start again.

Only when comes fairly easily and you feel more familiar with the flute, move on to:

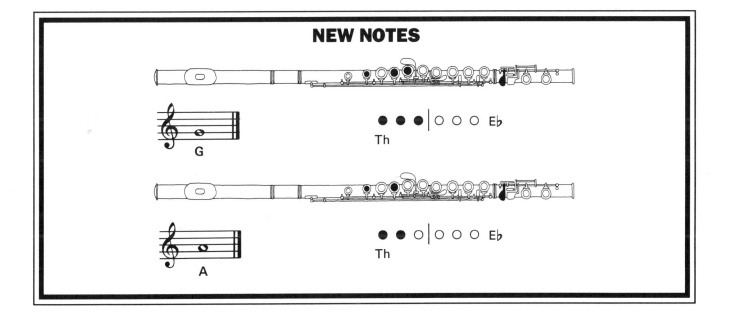

---

*(For the teacher). Although it is slightly more difficult to produce a sound from *D* than from the more usual beginners' notes, *B, A* and *G*, it is very much easier to hold the flute steady while playing *D*. This is important because many beginners are unable to sustain the left hand notes because they can't prevent the flute wobbling.

TIPS

1. Make sure your fingers are on the correct keys!

2. Never force the notes – don't expect a perfect sound straight away; your lips have to find the position that generates a good sound, and this takes time.

3. Practise, initially, in short bursts of five minutes or so.

What is the name of this note?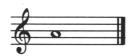

and this?

and this?

Now play them.

The count or beat is always steady, like a clock or metronome ticking. Count out loud
"**1, 2, 3, 4**" and keep repeating it.

♩ is a **minim** (some people call it a **half-note**), and it lasts for *two* counts or beats:

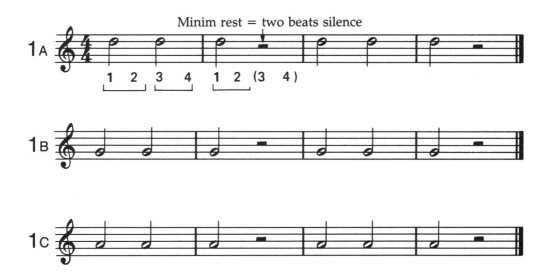

○ is a **semibreve** (or **whole-note**), and it lasts for *four* beats:
(If four beats are too long for you at the moment, return to this exercise when you reach the
end of Stage 1)

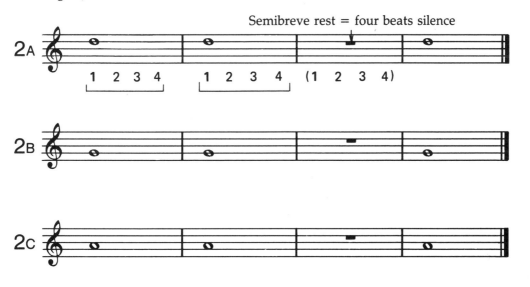

8

♩ is a **crotchet** (or **quarter-note**), and it lasts for *one* beat:

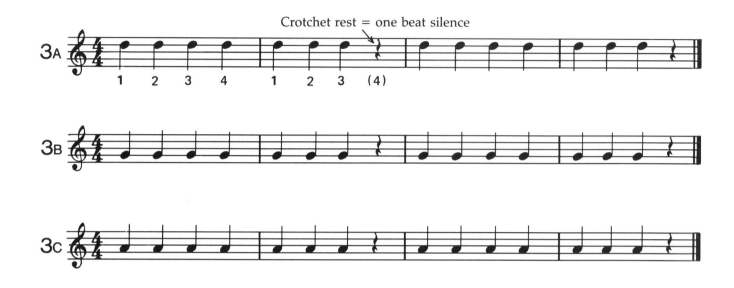

Start each note using your tongue (like saying "du"); this is called, not surprisingly, **tonguing**:

DATELINE D

G.L.

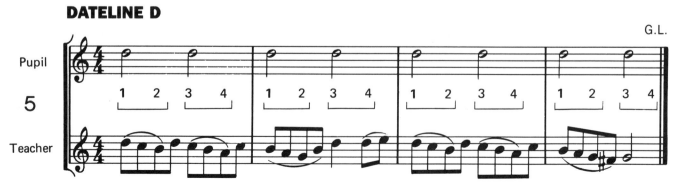

Try to keep going. Breathe when necessary, but if you have to cut short a note in order to take a breath, do not come in early on the next note.

It is very important to cultivate a steady (i.e. regular) sense of the beat – 1, 2, 3, 4 – going through your head as you play. If you can, listen to the other part and appreciate how your part fits with it.

For practice, these duets may also be played with a friendly pianist.

ASSIGNMENT A

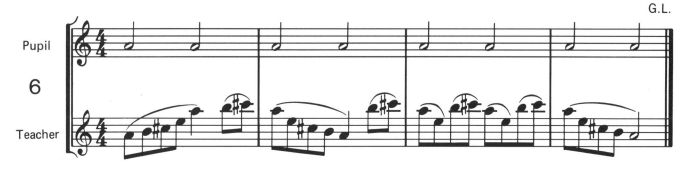

G-FORCE

STAGE 2

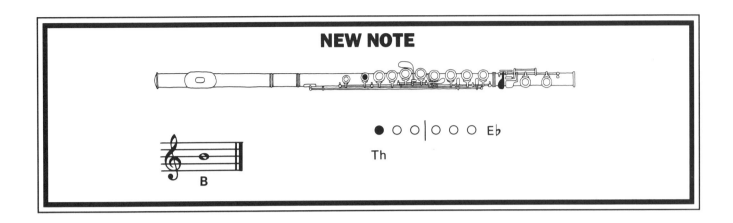

NEW NOTE

● ○ ○ | ○ ○ ○ E♭

Th

B

WIGWAM

G.L.

Pupil

1

Teacher

THREE BLIND MICE

2

AU CLAIR DE LA LUNE

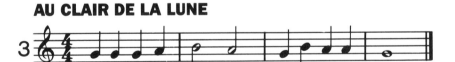

3

In the next pieces, not only play the right notes at the right time, but also try to enjoy fitting your part in with the well known tunes. This will help you to play *musically* as opposed to mechanically.

CAMPTOWN RACES

S. Foster (1826-64)

Pupil

4

Teacher

WHAT SHALL WE DO WITH A DRUNKEN SAILOR?

trad. sea shanty

* V is a breath mark

LI'L LIZA JANE

American trad.

12

Introducing the

NOTE RECOGNITION GAME

Get someone to time you: first of all **naming** the notes, and then **playing** them.*

7

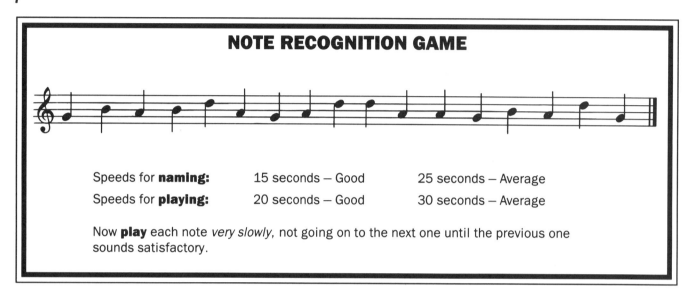

Clap the rhythms of No. 8. When you can do that, play the notes:

8

The **time signature** $\frac{3}{4}$ means three beats in each bar.

$\bullet$. is a **dotted minim** (or **dotted half-note**), and lasts for *three* beats:

COLONEL NUT

9

GENERAL CHAOS

10

---

*(For the teacher). Playing notes as fast as possible is very rarely a good idea. However, these *Note Recognition Games* work wonders in improving reading ability. Any harm done will be more than compensated for, if the pupil (as instructed) plays each note of the Game slowly.

REAR ADMIRAL BACKSLIDING

G.L.

SLURS

A **slur** (curved line) over or under a group of notes tells you to keep blowing steadily and to change the notes with *finger action only*. This means that the *first note only* of a slurred group is "tongued", but no other. Thus in No.12 tongue only the notes marked "Du".

MORSE CODE

CODE IN THE HEAD

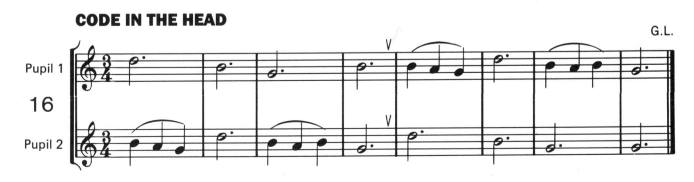

SOME SOUND ADVICE

A good sound on the flute will make anything you play pleasant, or even beautiful to listen to. The simplest folk tune played with good tone can give listeners (and yourself) a great deal of pleasure. However, good tone is not achieved overnight, but you can speed the process by being aware, *at all times*, of the sound that you are making.

Try playing one note (any note you like) for a complete breath. Do this several times, and each time really listen to the sound. If it doesn't please you, don't despair, you are only just beginning. Your tone is bound to improve over the weeks, *as long as you do not just play the pieces without thinking about the sound.*

If at any time you have trouble actually producing the notes as you play a piece, simply practise one note for a couple of minutes – trying to get that note as clear as you can – and then return to the piece.

What is this note called?

Listen to your sound.

Play it many times, each time for a whole breath.

Do the same with this note:  Again, listen to your sound.

And this:  Once again, listen to your sound!

STAGE 3

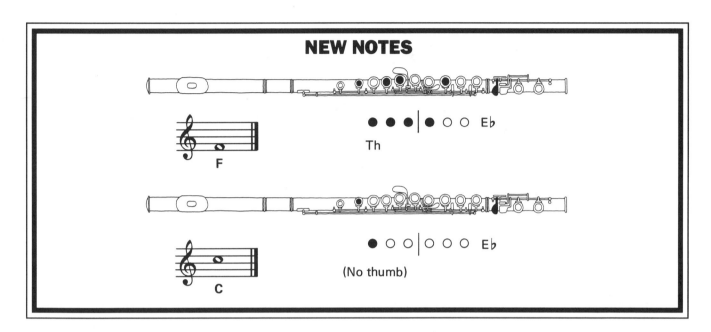

JINGLE BELL

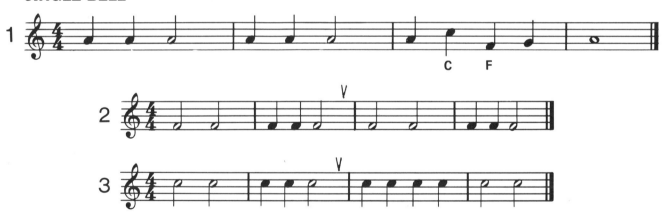

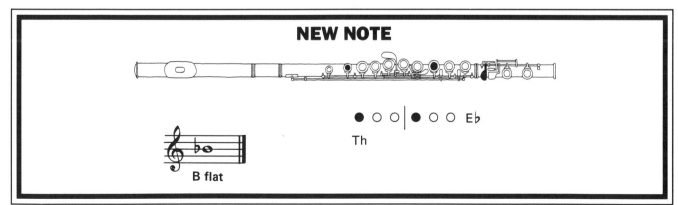

BEETHOVEN'S FIFTH SYMPHONY (extract)

NEW-NOTE PIECES

OLD MACDONALD

Farmyard song

THE BLUE DANUBE

J. Strauss II (1825-99)

Do you know the next tune? Play it accurately, and you should recognize it.

LONG NOTES ARE GOOD FOR YOU! Hold each note for a complete breath:

(Don't skip these – remember what I said about tone.)

SLUR PRACTICE

A WORD ABOUT BREATHING

There is absolutely no point in playing a piece while struggling for breath. Even if you have to breathe every bar it will sound better than if you are gasping for air all the time. However, music only makes sense if the pulse or beat is kept steady. If you run out of breath, cut a note short and breathe in the gap. Don't delay a new note.

In the pieces that do not have the breaths marked (V), put them in where it suits you; but if possible without interrupting the flow of the music.

DUETS FOR PUPIL AND TEACHER

15

NOTE RECOGNITION GAME

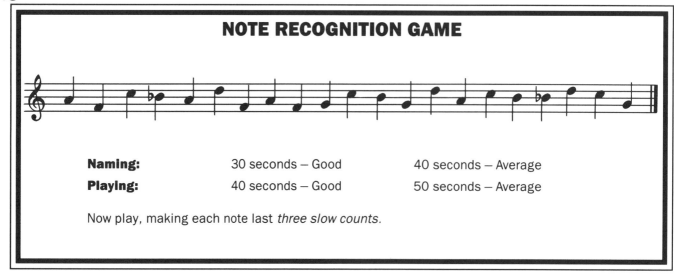

| Naming: | 30 seconds – Good | 40 seconds – Average |
| Playing: | 40 seconds – Good | 50 seconds – Average |

Now play, making each note last *three slow counts*.

TONGUING PRACTICE

ENGLISH FOOTBALL HOOLIGAN'S CHANT

16

Tie: *play as one note*

TIES

A **tie** is a curved line joining two notes on the *same* line or space. The lengths of the two notes are added together. Ties most often occur across a bar line.

WHEN THE SAINTS GO MARCHING IN

American traditional tune
now popular world-wide

17

MORE DUETS

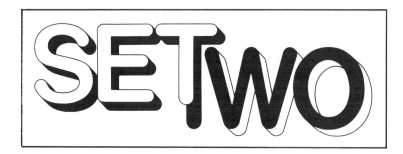

There are two volumes of teacher/pupil duets entitled 'Set Two' which make useful companion books to **'Take up the Flute'**. It is strongly recommended that they should be used in conjunction with this instruction book from this point on, as they contain many carefully graded and repetitive examples that help with particular problems of control and fingering. The pupil's parts are not difficult for the stage reached, but through repetition they hammer the problem (and its cure) home.

CHECKPOINT

You may think that you are getting on brilliantly. Well, the chances are that you are going through this book *too fast!* Go back to the beginning and play everything over again – *very carefully!*

1.   Listen to your tone.

2.   Make sure you play the right number of beats on each note, and observe the rests.

3.   Learn the tunes well enough to play them without stopping and starting.

4.   Be self-critical. Imagine your teacher is listening to you practise!

N.B. *Please refer back to this page as you progress through the book, and check that you are carrying out the points made here.*

STAGE 4

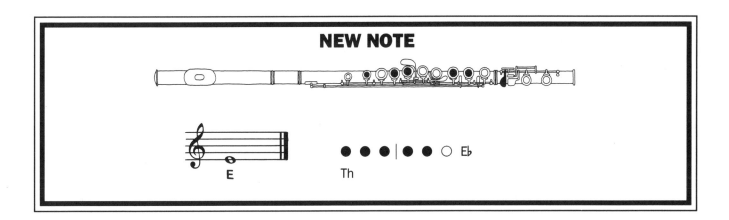

NEW NOTE

E   Th   ● ● ● | ● ● ○ E♭

1

2

FOLLOW ME DOWN

Pupil 1

3

Pupil 2

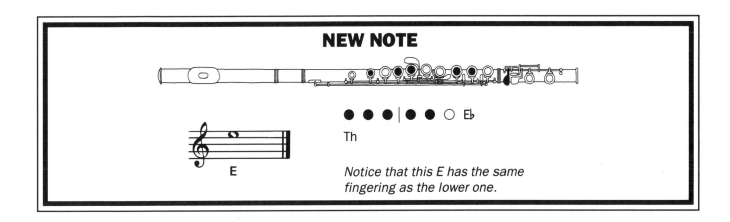

NEW NOTE

E   Th   ● ● ● | ● ● ○ E♭

Notice that this E has the same fingering as the lower one.

TWINKLE, TWINKLE LITTLE STAR

Lullaby derived from
an old French tune

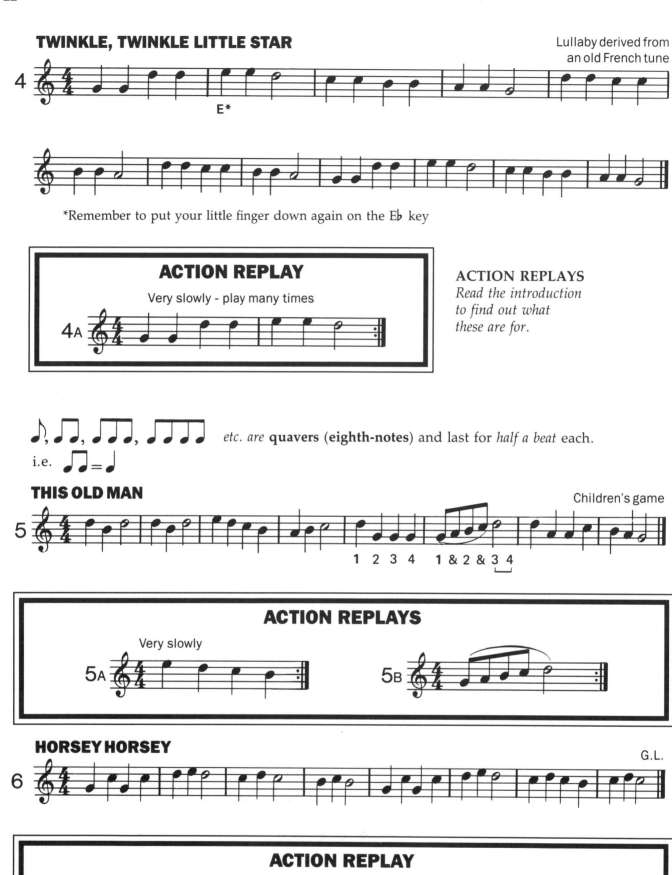

*Remember to put your little finger down again on the E♭ key

ACTION REPLAYS
*Read the introduction
to find out what
these are for.*

THIS OLD MAN

Children's game

HORSEY HORSEY

G.L.

Coming up are some well-known tunes. Some of the rhythmic patterns haven't yet been explained to you. If you know the pieces, all well and good; if not, leave them and come back to them later.

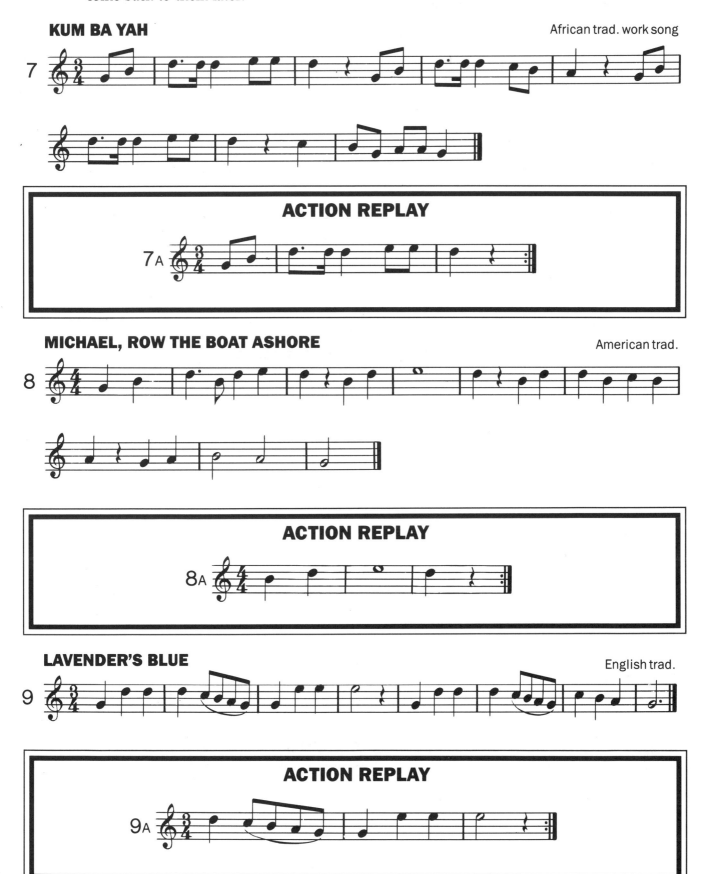

KUM BA YAH

African trad. work song

ACTION REPLAY

MICHAEL, ROW THE BOAT ASHORE

American trad.

ACTION REPLAY

LAVENDER'S BLUE

English trad.

ACTION REPLAY

OH SUSANNA!

Foster

10

1 2 3 4 &

ACTION REPLAY

10A   Slowly

IMPORTANT EXERCISES

11A

11B

11C

RHYTHM PRACTICE

Clap, then play

When you can *clap* these notes successfully, *play* them on **D** (as written), **B** and **A**, and then try them on both the **Low E** and **Higher E**.

Now go back and see if you can make a better job of the first few pieces.

13 SUMMERTIME

This very appealing melody contains many **Low** and **Higher E**s. Sing the tune through in your mind as you play. You are much more likely to produce the correct note if you hear it mentally first. You will probably have heard this tune before: if your version disagrees rhythmically with the one written here, feel free to play it as *you* know it:

You may find that the **Higher E** sometimes drops down to the lower one. If this happens too often, skip **Summertime** and come back to it at the end of Stage 5.

STAGE 5

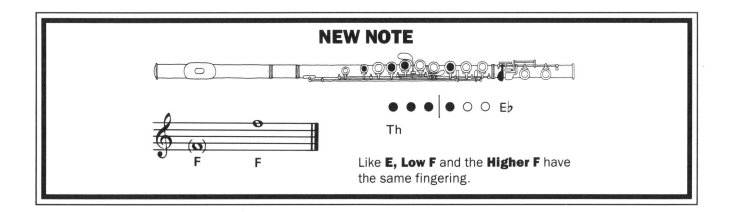

NEW NOTE

● ● ● | ● ○ ○ E♭

Th

Like **E, Low F** and the **Higher F** have the same fingering.

Practise changing from one **F** to the other. The secret is in the movement of the jaw. Practise moving your jaw forwards in an aggressive pose (keep the rest of your features serene!).

Blow a good **Low F**. Keep your lip position exactly the same and allow the jaw to move forward until you can get the **Higher F**. Always keep your jaw loose and ready to move forwards or backwards as required. Frequently waggle the jaw to make sure that it isn't rigid.

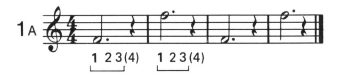

If you can't get the **Higher F**, don't worry; thousands have the same trouble at first! Try blowing slightly louder, but keep calm about it. The higher notes cannot be bullied into making an appearance; they have to be coaxed. They will come in time.

YANKEE DOODLE

American song

WE WISH YOU A MERRY CHRISTMAS

English trad.

4

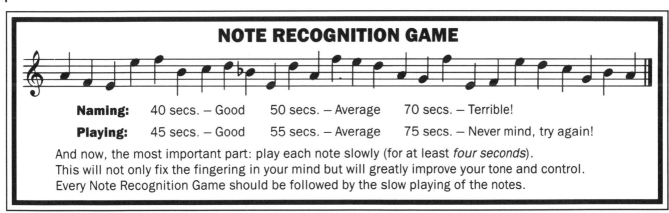

INTERMEZZO

J. Brahms (1833-97)

28

You have recently been playing some familiar tunes and your knowledge of them helps you to get them right. Here are three tunes you won't know (because I made them up myself!). You will have to work them out using your note recognition and rhythm skills. Eventually they should sound just as familiar as the other tunes.

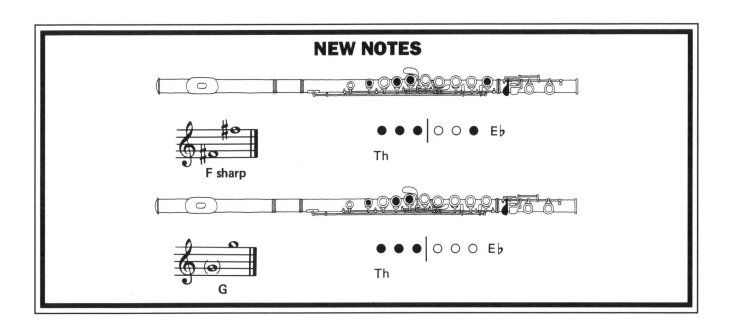

GOD SAVE THE QUEEN

If you feel uncomfortable playing the higher notes, think on this: one of the most common reasons for high note failure is general tenseness and anxiety. These can cause your breathing and your jaw muscles to become rigid. (Imagine yourself in a scary situation and think what happens to your breath and face). So . . .

1. Approach the high notes quite freely. Genuinely don't mind if you fail; you can try and try again.

2. Constantly check that you are breathing freely and that your jaw is loose.

LOOSE JAW

THE FIRST NOWELL

ACTION REPLAYS

STAGE 6
GETTING USED TO THE ♩.

You have already played some dotted crotchets (dotted quarter-notes) in **Oh Susanna**, **God save the Queen** and **The First Nowell**. Here are some more very well known tunes with plenty of ♩.s:

SKYE BOAT SONG — Lullaby from the Isle of Skye — FINE *(End)* — **D.C. al Fine**

(Play from the beginning once more; stop at 'FINE')

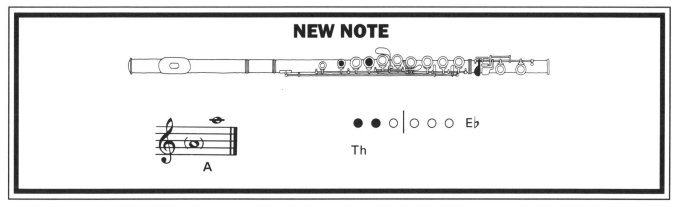

NEW NOTE

ONCE IN ROYAL DAVID'S CITY — H. J. Gauntlett (1805-76)

ACTION REPLAY REMINDER

Action Replays are a vital part of this book. They should be played slowly, evenly and *correctly*, and, of course, repeated at least three times. If you make mistakes in them, you are playing them *too fast*. They should be played at half the normal speed of the piece they come from. If you still cannot manage to play them, you have gone through the book too quickly and will have to return to a stage in which you *can* play the pieces comfortably. If this is necessary, don't resent it; it will help you greatly to go over the same material again.

32

EINE KLEINE NACHT MUSIK

W.A. Mozart (1756-91)

AULD LANG SYNE

Scots song, traditionally
sung at the New Year

EXPLAINING THE DOT

A dot after a note always makes it last longer.

♩. = 3 beats instead of 2;   o· = 6 beats instead of 4.

You add on to the note *half of its own value:* e.g.   ♩. = ♩ + ♩
                                                        1 2 3   1 2 3

So ♩. = 1½ beats ♩ + ♪ (1 + half of 1);   o· = 6 beats o + ♩ (4 + half of 4).

RHYTHM PRACTICE

Clap, then play:

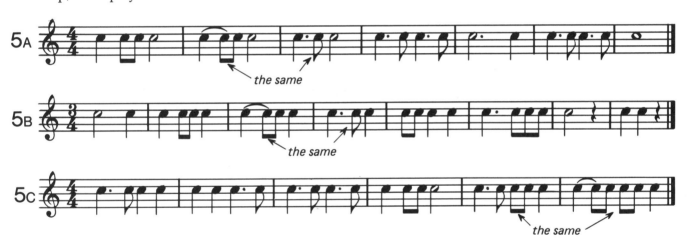

The next tune has exactly the same rhythm as **Auld Lang Syne**, but has different *notes:*

'LANG SYNE AULD'

G.L.

Now here are the notes of **Auld Lang Syne** to a different *rhythm:*

'SYNE LANG AULD'

Look carefully at Nos. 8 and 9 and play them accurately:

DOTTY OLD CROTCHET

CROTCHETY OLD DOT

Use the rhythms of **Skye Boat Song** to help you with Nos. 10 and 11.

SCOOT BY SONG

ANDANTE GRAZIOSO

STAGE 7

You will have noticed (I hope!) that high notes and low notes often have the same fingering. If the higher notes still tend to drop down, blow them a bit louder for now. When (with practice) you have found out how to get these notes on demand (a combination of breath control and small jaw movement), you will find it easier to play them quietly.

The next tune will help you with this. It is in the **Key** of **G**, which has the **Key Signature** of **F sharp**: all **F**s are automatically sharpened. (Keys and Key Signatures will be fully explained in Book 2.)

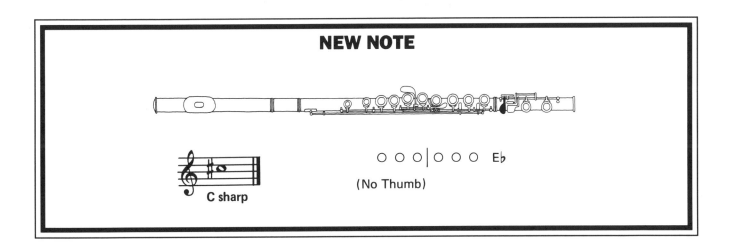

OVER THE RAINBOW

Harold Arlen (b. 1905)

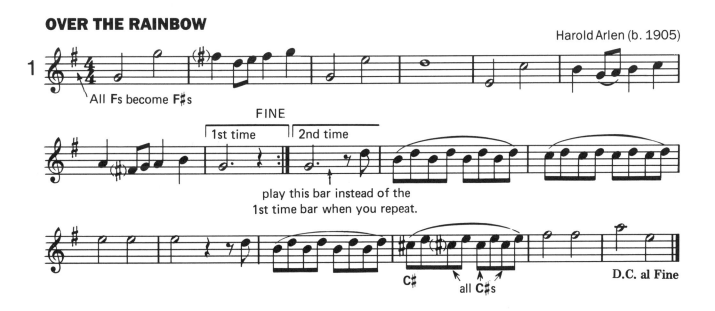

Spend time learning to play this attractive melody really smoothly and expressively. It covers the range of notes learnt so far; it has long notes for tone practice and provides excellent finger practice across the registers.

2

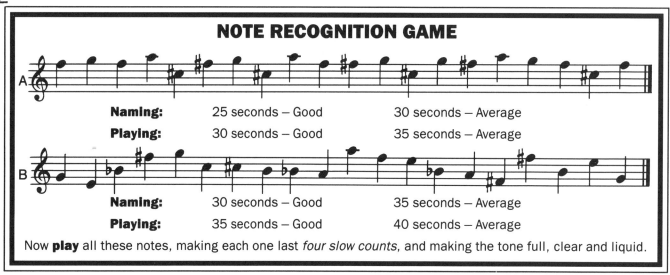

NOTE RECOGNITION GAME

Naming:	25 seconds – Good	30 seconds – Average
Playing:	30 seconds – Good	35 seconds – Average

Naming:	30 seconds – Good	35 seconds – Average
Playing:	35 seconds – Good	40 seconds – Average

Now **play** all these notes, making each one last *four slow counts*, and making the tone full, clear and liquid.

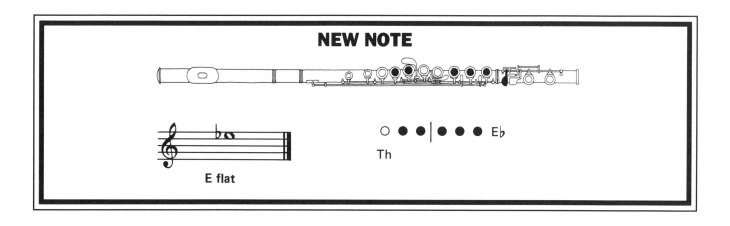

NEW NOTE

E flat

Th   Eb

JINGLE BELLS

J. Pierpont

3

all Ebs

all Ebs

LIGHTLY ROW

ACCIDENTALS

A sharp (♯) *raises* the pitch of a note by a semitone.
Play **F**, then **F sharp**; **C**, then **C sharp**.

A flat (♭) *lowers* the note by a semitone.
Play **B**, then **B flat**; **E,** then **E flat**.

A natural sign (♮) restores any altered note to its original pitch; a natural will cancel a flat or sharp. Collectively, sharps, flats and naturals are called **accidentals**.

Accidentals make the same notes in the same bar follow suit thus:

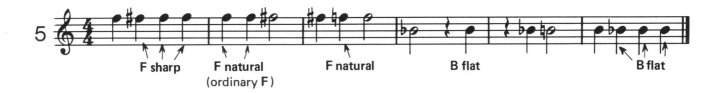

Work out which **E**s are flat and which natural, and then play them:

Accidentals at the beginning of each line of music define the key of that music.
They tell you which notes of the piece will be sharpened or flattened.

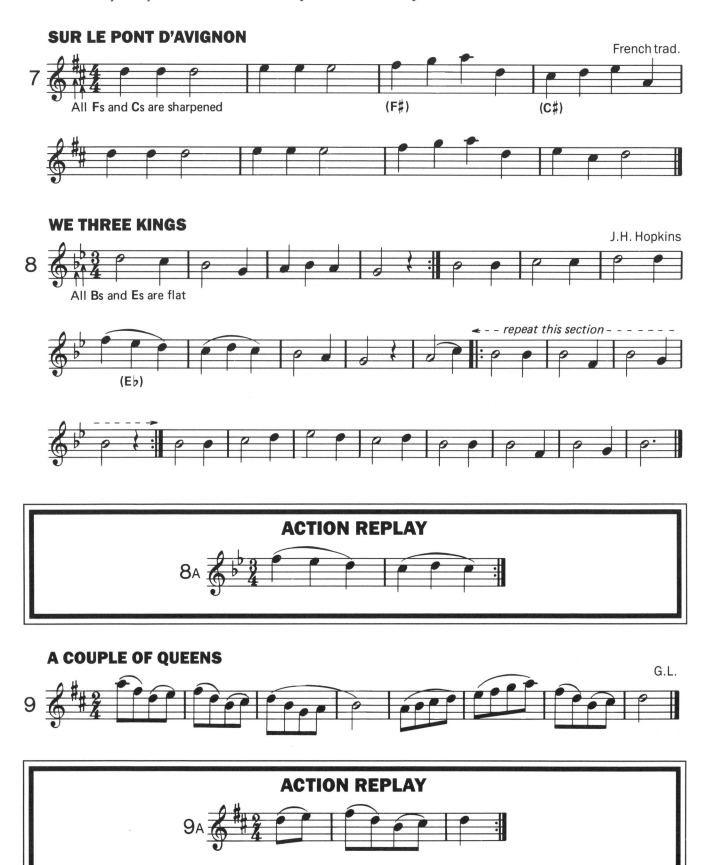

SUR LE PONT D'AVIGNON

French trad.

7

All **F**s and **C**s are sharpened

(F♯)   (C♯)

WE THREE KINGS

J.H. Hopkins

8

All **B**s and **E**s are flat

(E♭)

← - - repeat this section - - - - - -

ACTION REPLAY

8A

A COUPLE OF QUEENS

G.L.

9

ACTION REPLAY

9A

10

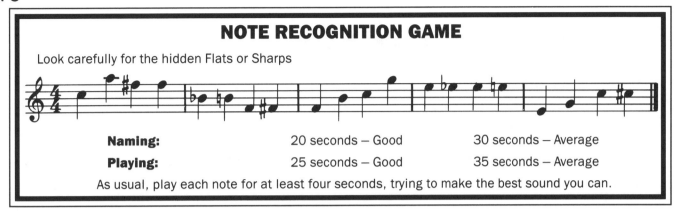

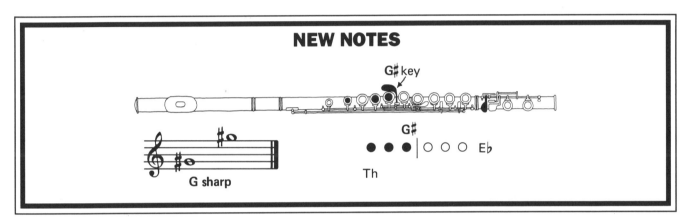

GREENSLEEVES

English trad.

SLEIGH RIDE

S. Prokofiev (1891-1953)

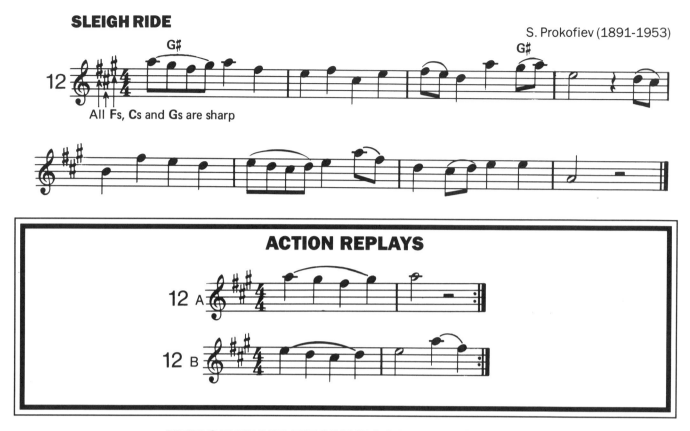

All **Fs**, **Cs** and **Gs** are sharp

IMPORTANT TECHNICAL PRACTICE

Play these exercises until you are sick of them – and then play them again! Try to move smoothly from one slurred note to another.

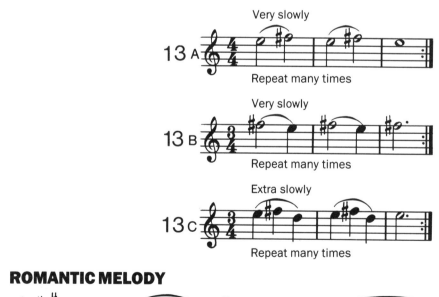

ROMANTIC MELODY

A. Borodin (1833-87)

Fs, Cs & Gs sharpened

STAGE 8

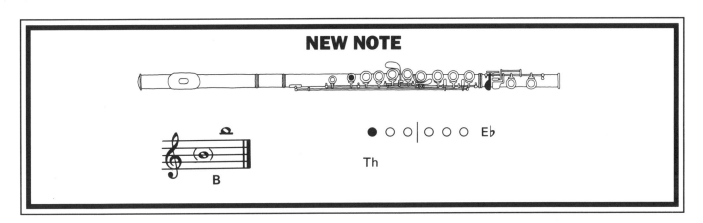

NEW NOTE

YOU ARE MY SUNSHINE

David & Mitchell

(Breathe here)

1

All **F**s and **C**s sharpened

BRANLE

J.B. de Boismortier (1689-1755)

2

Pupil 1

Pupil 2

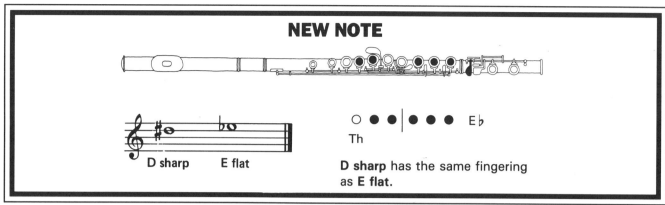

NEW NOTE

D sharp   E flat

D sharp has the same fingering as E flat.

D sharp has the same fingering as E flat – in other words it is the same note! If this sounds like "Double Dutch", ask a friendly pianist to explain (it is easier on the piano).

FANTASY IMPROMPTU

Slowly and expressively   F. Chopin (1810-49)

3

HAVA NAGILA (in part)

Israeli trad.

4

GAVOTTE (from **French Suite No.5**)   J.S. Bach (1685-1750)

5

ACTION REPLAYS

5A Very slowly   5B Slowly   5C Slowly

Repeat many times   Many times   Many times

43

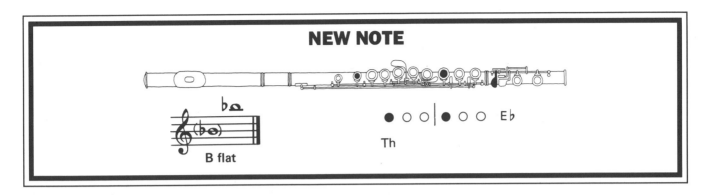

44

COCKLES AND MUSSELS

Irish trad.

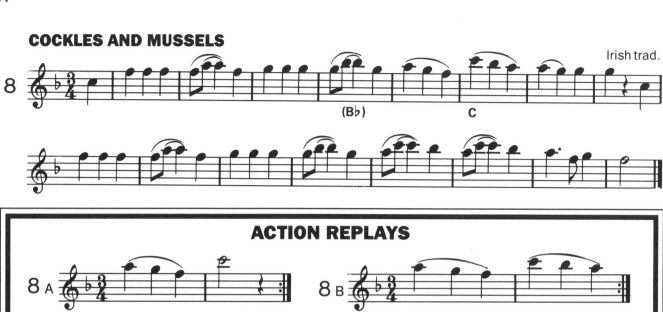

(B♭)   C

ACTION REPLAYS

8 A   8 B

RHYTHM PRACTICE

Clap, then play:

9 A

9 B

9 C

9 D

10

NOTE RECOGNITION GAME

(Recent notes)

Naming:	25 seconds – Good	35 seconds – Average
Playing:	30 seconds – Good	40 seconds – Average

Play each note *slowly* for tone practice.

Pupil 1

11

Pupil 2

G.L.

SYMPHONY No. 40 (extract)

Mozart

12

Perhaps you are having trouble with the **Higher B flat, B** and **C**. In which case play through the next exercises a number of times.

Take a fairly large breath at the beginning of each of these exercises and hold the top note for as long as your breath lasts – *even if the note drops down an octave.*

It is important (and easier) to slur up to the top note.

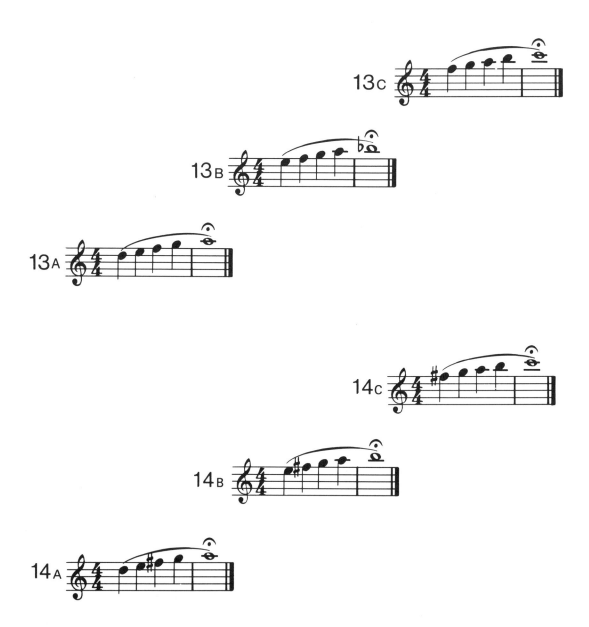

If you can hold on to the high notes without strain, try the pieces again. If not, go on to the next stage, and then return to this one.

STAGE 9

The jaw should be drawn further back for low notes. Don't strain for them. Try hard to get them without becoming anxious.

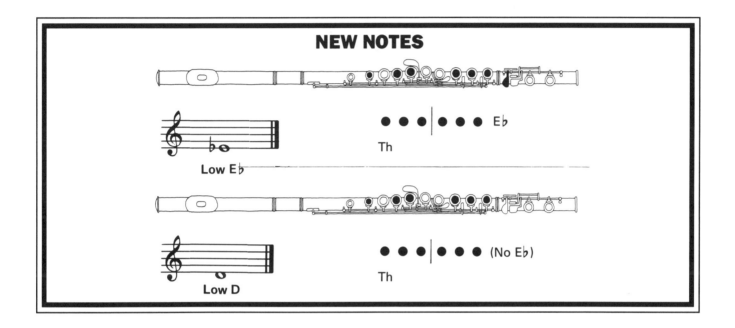

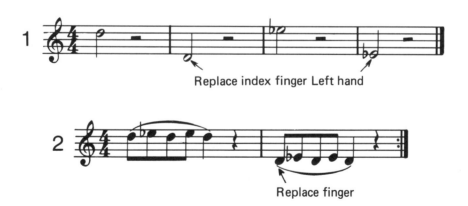

Replace index finger Left hand

Replace finger

FOLLOW ME DOWN (again)

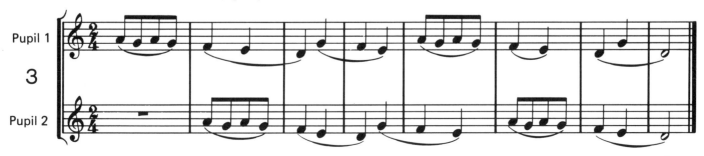

FOLLOW ME DOWN (once more)

Compare the sound of Nos. 3 and 4. The notes are practically the same, but the *key signature* has altered. This makes a world of difference. Key signatures are fully explained in Book 2.

Learn to play these well known tunes from memory:

CLEMENTINE

American miners' song

GOD REST YOU MERRY, GENTLEMEN

Old English Christmas carol

---

*Semiquavers (♪, ♫ etc.) are explained in Book 2. Meanwhile play *Clementine* how you think it goes.

NEW NOTES

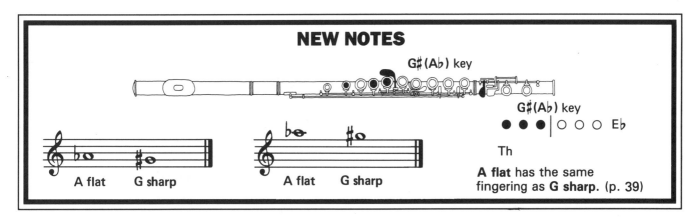

G♯(A♭) key

G♯(A♭) key

● ● ● | ○ ○ ○ E♭

Th

A flat has the same fingering as **G sharp**. (p. 39)

A flat   G sharp   A flat   G sharp

CAN-CAN

J. Offenbach (1819-80)

7

A♭

1.   2.

ACTION REPLAYS

7A

7B

LA CUCURACHA

Mexican song

8

A♭

ACTION REPLAYS

8A

8B

50

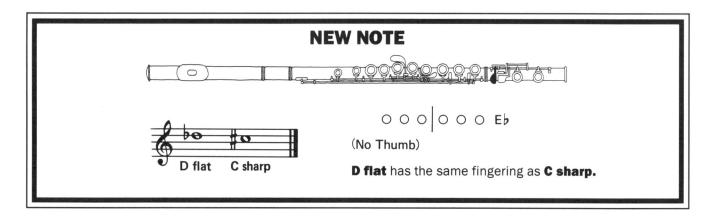

NEW NOTE

○ ○ ○ | ○ ○ ○ E♭

(No Thumb)

D flat has the same fingering as **C sharp**.

D flat   C sharp

The next tune is quite a challenge. It has a key signature of four flats. Every **B**, **E**, **A** and **D** will be flattened. Before you start the tune, play those flats.

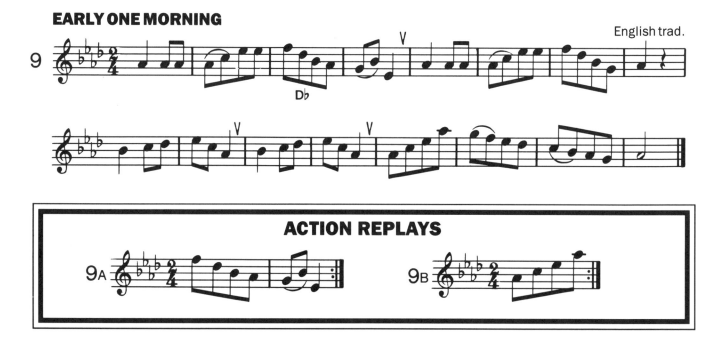

EARLY ONE MORNING

English trad.

ACTION REPLAYS

It is not easy to produce low notes at all loudly on the flute. The next exercises should strengthen your sound down low. Naturally, playing them once through will not do the trick – nor will playing them solidly for an hour. Just include them in your regular practice and the low notes will improve as your general flute playing improves.

Play **Low G** repeatedly until the tone improves, then:

Complete breath

Hold the last note of each slur for a complete breath, and repeat each group.

STAGE 10
PLAYING IN BOTH REGISTERS

Here are some simple tunes. Play them many times in the low register until you are thoroughly familiar with them – and then take them up to the high register. See if you can change from one register to the other at will:

AU CLAIR DE LA LUNE (low)

French trad.

AU CLAIR DE LA LUNE (high)

SKIP TO MY LOU (low)

American trad.

SKIP TO MY LOU (high)

LAVENDER'S BLUE (low)

English trad.

LAVENDER'S BLUE (high)

Here is **Old MacDonald** in two keys and two registers:

OLD MACDONALD HAD A FARM (in G & A♭)

English trad.

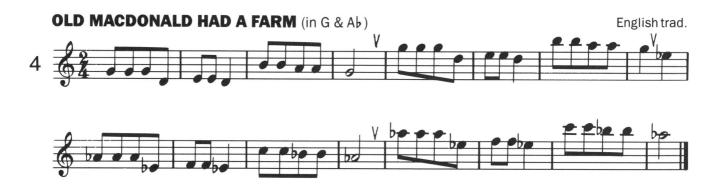

Some of you may find these tunes too childish. However, switching from one register to another on the flute is never easy, and if you know the tune you are supposed to be playing, you are half-way there.

Now, by way of contrast, here is an unfamiliar tune. The fingering is no more difficult than some of the nursery rhymes; but because you don't have the sound of the tune in your head, you will probably find it harder to play. Try to prove me wrong!

FLEUR DE LYS (low)

G.L.

FLEUR DE LYS (high)

Now write a tune yourself that can be played in both registers. Naturally keep it simple and within a range of no more than six notes. (Did you know you were a composer?).

LOW REGISTER

HIGH REGISTER

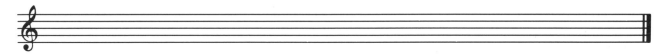

QUIZ

"Notes with the same fingering"

The note in between **G** and **A** can be called either **G sharp** or **A flat**; between **D** and **E** the note is either **D sharp** or **E flat**.

What else, besides **B flat**, can you call the note in between **A** and **B**? Similarly, what is the name, besides **F sharp**, for the note between **F** and **G**?

Which notes have the same fingering as:

Eb = D♯   ; Gb =   ; C♯ =   ; Db =   ; Ab =   ;

A♯ =   ; Bb =   ; G♯ =   ; F♯ =   ?   (The first one is done for you).

Write (in music) the equivalent note to the first one in each bar; again, the first one has been done for you.

Here are all the notes you have learnt in this book, written out in sequence, up and down:

This is known as the **Chromatic Scale**. Play it extremely carefully, making sure you don't miss out any notes. If you cannot remember one of the notes, think, first of all, whether that note has another name with which you are more familiar. If you are still unsure, return to the Stage in which that note first appears and play through all the pieces there that contain the note.

Finally play this Chromatic Scale, both tongued and slurred, every time you practise. Try to achieve a satisfying and even flow.

You are now ready to move on to Book 2. Some good tunes are waiting for you!

COPYRIGHT ACKNOWLEDGEMENTS

OVER THE RAINBOW (p.35)

Words by E.Y. Harburg. Music by Harold Arlen.

© 1938, 1939 (Renewed 1966, 1967) Metro-Goldwyn-Mayer Inc. All rights controlled and administered by Leo Feist, Inc., a catalogue of CBS Songs, a Division of CBS Inc. International Copyright Secured. All Rights Reserved. Used by permission.

SUMMERTIME (p.25)

Words by Du Bosé Heyward. Music by George Gershwin.

© Copyright 1935 by Gershwin Publishing Corporation. Copyright Renewed, Assigned to Chappell and Co. Inc. International copyright secured. All rights reserved.
Used by permission of:- Hal Leonard Publishing Corporation / Chappell & Co (Australia) Pty Ltd / Chappell & Co Holland B.V. / Intersong-Förlagen AB / AB Carl Gehrmans Musikförlag / Chappell Music Ltd, London

YOU ARE MY SUNSHINE (p.41)

Reprinted by permission of:- Southern Music Publishing Co. Ltd / Holland Music B.V. / Southern Music Espanola, S.A. / Southern Music Belgium / Southern Music AG, Switzerland / Société D'Editions Musicales Internationales / Peer-Southern Organisation, Canada / Southern Music AB, Stockholm / Southern Music Publishing Co (Australasia) Pty Ltd / Peer Musikverlag GmbH / Peer-Southern Organisation Tokyo

FINGERING CHART

Here, for easy reference, are all the notes that you have learnt in this book.

The page numbers tell you where the notes were first introduced.

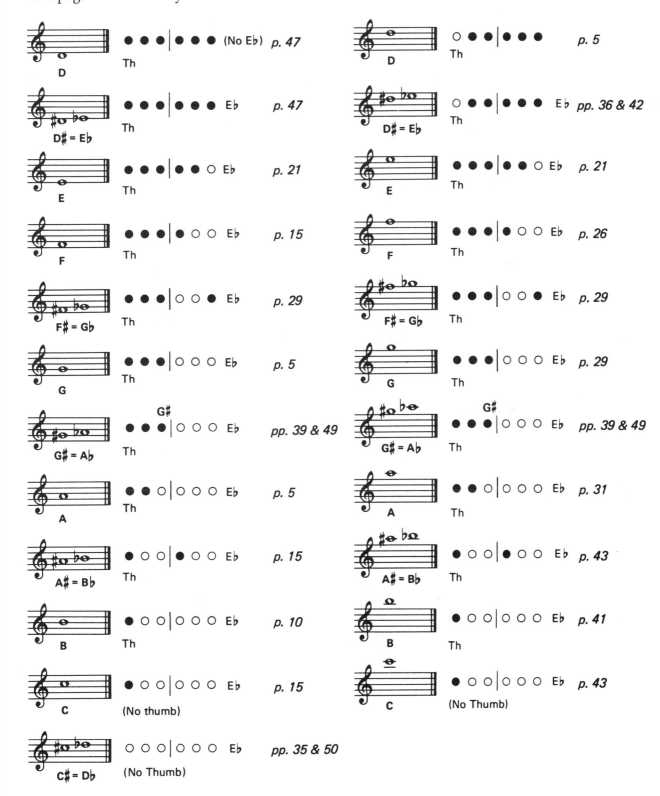

KALEIDOSCOPE
Easy music for varied ensembles

SUPER SOUNDS
FOR SCHOOL INSTRUMENTAL GROUPS
LARGE OR SMALL

Chester Music is proud to present a brand new series of individual pieces specially developed to meet the need for **easy music, carefully written for each instrument**, which will sound **effective with any instrumental combination** whatever the size and make up of the group.

The following titles have been published so far, each one issued complete with score and set of 48 parts:

1. **OOM-PAH-PAH**
   from **Oliver** (Lionel Bart)
2. **TOURDION**
   a 16th century French Dance
3. **MEMORY**
   from **Cats** (Andrew Lloyd Webber)
4. **HELLO** (Lionel Richie)
5. **POMP AND CIRCUMSTANCE**
   (Edward Elgar)
6. **JUPITER** (Gustav Holst)
7. **THE SOUND OF SILENCE**
   (Paul Simon)
8. **BEHOLD THE LORD HIGH EXECUTIONER!**
   from **The Mikado** (Arthur Sullivan)
9. **THE SNOWMAN** (Howard Blake)
10. **HALLELUJAH CHORUS**
    from **The Messiah** (G.F. Handel)
11. **IMAGINE** (John Lennon)
12. **STAR WARS** (John Williams)
13. **THE BLUE DANUBE** (J. Strauss II)
14. **SWEDISH RHAPSODY** (Hugo Alfvén)

15. **BRIGHT EYES** (Mike Batt)
16. **RUDOLPH THE RED-NOSED REINDEER** (Johnny Marks)
17. **DANSERYE**
    Two Renaissance Dances
    (Tylman Susato)
18. **THE BARE NECESSITIES**
    from **The Jungle Book**
    (Terry Gilkyson)
19. **LOCH LOMOND** (Scottish Air)
20. **A WHITER SHADE OF PALE**
    (Procul Harum)
21. **CORONATION STREET**
    (Eric Spear)
22. **So here it is MERRY CHRISTMAS EVERYBODY** (Slade)
23. **ROCK AROUND THE CLOCK**
    (Bill Haley)
24. **SAILING** (Rod Stewart)
25. **SUMMERTIME**
    from **Porgy & Bess** (George Gershwin)

26. **Autumn** and **Winter** themes from **THE SEASONS** (Antonio Vivaldi)
27. **MATCH OF THE DAY** (Rhet Stoller)
28. **CHARIOTS OF FIRE** (Vangelis)
29. **MARY'S BOY CHILD** (Jester Hairston)
30. **CHRISTMAS BONANZA**
    Seven Favourite Carols
31. **PIE JESU** (Andrew Lloyd Webber)
32. **A HARD DAY'S NIGHT**
    (Lennon & McCartney)
33. **NEIGHBOURS** (Hatch & Trent)
34. **LUCY IN THE SKY WITH DIAMONDS** (Lennon & McCartney)
35. **YESTERDAY**
    (Lennon & McCartney)
36. **EASTENDERS** (Osbourne & May)
37. **YELLOW SUBMARINE**
    (Lennon & McCartney)

Further titles, from classics to pops, will be issued regularly.

CHESTER MUSIC
(A division of Music Sales Limited)
8/9 Frith Street, London W1V 5TZ

Flute   Editor: Trevor Wye   Clarinet   Editor: Thea King

Oboe   Editor: James Brown   Bassoon   Editor: William Waterhouse

Saxophone   Editor: Paul Harvey

A growing collection of volumes from Chester Music, containing a
wide range of pieces from different periods.

FLUTE SOLOS VOLUME I

Baston	Siciliana from Concertino in D
Blavet	Gavotte—La Dédale
Bochsa	Nocturne
Buchner	Russian Melody from Fantasy op. 22
Eichner	Minuet from Sonata No. 6
Franck	Intrada
Franck	Galliard
Lichtenthal	Theme
Mozart	Minuets I & II from Sonata No. 1
Paisiello	Nel Cor Più
Vivaldi	Andante from Sonata No. 3 of The Faithful Shepherd
Vivaldi	Pastorale from Sonata No. 4 of The Faithful Shepherd

FLUTE SOLOS VOLUME II

Blavet	Les Tendres Badinages from Sonata No. 6
Chopin	A Rossini Theme
Donjon	Adagio Nobile
Eichner	Scherzando from Sonata No. 6
Harmston	Andante
Jacob	Cradle Song from Five Pieces for Harmonica and Piano
Mozart	Minuets I & II from Sonata No. 5
Mozart	Allegro from Sonata in G
Pauli	Capriccio
Telemann	Tempo Giusto from Sonata in D minor
Vivaldi	Allegro from Sonata No. 2 of The Faithful Shepherd

FLUTE SOLOS VOLUME III

Blavet	Sicilienne from Sonata No. 4	Loeillet	Gavotte and Aria from Sonata No. 7
Blavet	Les Regrets from Sonata No. 5	Nørgard	Andantino—Pastorale
Donjon	Offertoire op. 12	Sibelius	Solo from Scaramouche op. 71
Eichner	Allegro from Sonata No. 6	Telemann	Grave from Sonata in G minor
Kelly	Jig from Serenade	Vivaldi	Largo from Sonata No. 6 of The Faithful Shepherd

Also available: FLUTE DUETS AND TRIOS
Further details on request

CHESTER MUSIC

(A Music Sales Limited Company)
8/9 Frith Street, London, W1V 5TZ

WOODWIND ENSEMBLES

A series which offers
MAXIMUM FLEXIBILITY
in relation to

* students' varied
  technical abilities
* instrumentation
* number of players
* range of music

ENSEMBLES POUR BOIS

Une série offrant un
**MAXIMUM DE CHOIX D'ADAP-
TATIONS** en fonction des

* divers aptitudes
  techniques des étudiants
* de l'instrumentation
* du nombre d'exécutants
* de la musique choisie

HOLZBLÄSER ENSEMBLES

Eine Reihe mit
**GRÖSSTER VARIATIONS-
BREITE** in bezug auf

* den unterschiedlichen
  Standard der Schüler
* die instrumentation
* die Anzahl der Spieler
* die Auswahl an Musik

CONJUNTOS DE VIENTO

Una colección que ofrece
MAXIMA FLEXIBILIDAD
en cuanto a:

* estudiantes de diferentes
  grados de experiencia
* instrumentación
* número de instrumentistas
* repertorio musical

木管アンサンブル

このシリーズは
以下の様な目的のために
最大限の適応性をもっている:

★生徒の様々な
  技量に応して
★楽器編成に応して
★演奏者の数に応して
★豊富なレパートリとして

CHESTER MUSIC

(A Music Sales Limited Company)
8/9 Frith Street, London, W1V 5TZ
Exclusive distributors: Music Sales Ltd., Newmarket Road
Bury St Edmunds, Suffolk. IP33 3YB